LETTER TO THE WORLD

The Life and Dances of
MARTHA GRAHAM

by Trudy Garfunkel

 Little, Brown and Company
Boston   New York   Toronto   London

To Jared, Matthew, and Maren
And in memory of Merrie Miller

◆

First Edition

Title page illustration: Martha Graham in *Letter to the World* (1940). Drawing by Charlotte Trowbridge.

Illustration credits: Pages 11 and 45: collection of the author. Pages 31, 32, and 34: photographs by Soichi Sunami; Dance Collection, the New York Public Library for the Performing Arts; Astor, Lenox, and Tilden Foundations; courtesy Reiko Kopelson. Pages 36, 50, and 54: photographs copyright 1941 by Barbara Morgan. Page 43: photograph by Jun Miki; courtesy of the Isamu Noguchi Foundation, Inc. Page 57: photograph courtesy of the American Foundation for the Blind, Helen Keller Archives, and Helen Keller International. Page 64: photograph by Arnold Eagle. Pages 83 and 85: © 1993 Martha Swope. All other images are courtesy of the Dance Collection, the New York Public Library for the Performing Arts; Astor, Lenox, and Tilden Foundations.

The author is grateful for permission to use the following copyrighted material: "Martha Graham," by James Laughlin, from *The Collected Poems of James Laughlin*. By permission of Moyer Bell, Wakefield, Rhode Island.

Library of Congress Cataloging-in-Publication Data

Garfunkel, Trudy.
    Letter to the world : the life and dances of Martha Graham / by Trudy
Garfunkel: — 1st ed.
        p.   cm.
    Includes bibliographical references and index.
    ISBN 0-316-30413-1
       1. Graham, Martha — Juvenile literature. 2. Dancers — United States — Biography —
Juvenile literature. 3. Choreographers — United States — Biography — Juvenile literature.
[1. Graham, Martha. 2. Dancers. 3. Modern dance — Biography.] I. Title.
GV1785.G7G37   1995
792.8'028'092 — dc20
[B]   94-16715

10 9 8 7 6 5 4 3 2 1

HAWK

Published simultaneously in Canada by Little, Brown & Company (Canada) Limited

Printed in the United States of America

CONTENTS

◆

MARTHA GRAHAM

◆

Earth and water air
and fire her body

beats the ground it
flows it floats it

seems to burn she
burns herself away

until there is no
body there at all

but only the pure
elements moving as

music moves moving
from her into us

—*James Laughlin*

PROLOGUE

◆

Dance is a language, a way of communicating without words. It is a language that can not only tell a story but also convey emotions. Dance can be entertainment, a form of religious observance, or a part of social occasions. But no matter how dance communicates, its vocabulary is not words and sentences but steps, movements, and patterns.

Many dance vocabularies are very old. Some African and Asian dances have been performed in the same way for more than two thousand years. The basic steps and movements of classical ballet were developed over three hundred years ago in the royal courts of Europe. We don't always know who created the older dance styles, but we now have a name for the people who carefully structure and plan dance steps and movements so they can be repeated and performed by others. They are called choreographers. Choreographers may adapt or change older dance forms, but most new styles of dancing are at least based on what has come before. It is rare for one person to invent a dance vocabulary that is unique.

However, in 1894, a little girl was born in Pennsylvania who would grow up to do what few people before her or since have done—create a radically new way of dancing. She invented a technique with its own vocabulary of steps and movements that would change the world of dance. Her career would span more than seventy years, and she would become America's most renowned dancer, hailed around the world not only for her choreography but for her far-ranging influence on theatrical costumes and set design as well. For the originality and scope of her work, she would be called a genius.

That little girl was Martha Graham (1894–1991), and surprisingly, she was born into a world where dancing professionally on the stage was something that proper young ladies just did not do.

CHAPTER ONE
Beginnings

◆

Martha Graham, one of the great creative artists of the twentieth century, was born on May 11, 1894, in Allegheny, Pennsylvania. Her father, the blond and dashing George Greenfield Graham, was a doctor who treated mental and emotional disorders. Today he would be called a psychiatrist, but one hundred years ago, that term was not yet used, and his specialty was considered unusual for a small-town physician. Dr. Graham's Scotch-Irish grandfather had emigrated to America in the early years of the nineteenth century. He had arrived in the United States penniless but had eventually founded Pittsburgh's first bank. Martha's mother, Jane (Jenny) Beers Graham, was delicate, pretty, and soft-spoken. A tenth-generation American, she was a direct descendant of Miles Standish and could trace her family back to the Pilgrims who came to America on the *Mayflower*.

Martha, whose name means lady or "mistress of the house," was

George Graham, Martha's father (c. 1893)   Jenny Graham, Martha's mother (c. 1893)

the oldest of three sisters. Although she was considered plain as a child, Martha resembled her mother in that both were petite and had shiny black hair. From her father she inherited an iron determination and stubborn temper. She would display these personality traits throughout her life. As an adult, she would admit that she had been a difficult child who was always getting into trouble.

Martha's middle sister, Mary, was born in 1896; the baby, Georgia (called Geordie), in 1900. A brother, born in 1906, died at the age of two from measles. Eventually the Graham household also included Lizzie Prendergast, a maid, nurse, and nanny who lived with the family for many years. An orphan from Ireland, she had been a patient of Dr. Graham; he had saved her life when she was bitten by a pack of wild dogs. Shortly afterward, she arrived at the Grahams' doorstep insisting she had come to take care of the doctor's family in gratitude for his help.

The Graham family was well off and lived in a big, comfortable house. But Allegheny (now a part of Pittsburgh) was located in the heart of Pennsylvania's coal country. It was a bleak, gray mill town that Martha later described as "spun entirely out of evening and dark thread." It was impossible to stay clean in Allegheny. No matter how freshly washed clothing was in the morning, by nighttime it was black, covered in soot. Coal dust and ashes were everywhere. To protect their skin, women and girls wore veils and cotton gloves whenever they went outside.

The world into which Martha Graham was born was proper, orderly, and straightlaced. It was a time called the Victorian age, named after the British queen Victoria, whose sense of decorum

Martha, two years old (1896)

and morality set the tone for polite behavior in England and America for the second half of the nineteenth century.

Martha's upbringing reflected the strict and disciplined outlook of the Victorian era, a time when good manners were as important as good morals. The girls were not allowed outside unchaperoned. They always had to be properly dressed, down to their immaculate white gloves. They were expected to be respectful and truthful and to act with decorum at all times. For the Graham children, weekdays meant school, homework, and study. Sundays were devoted to church, Sunday School, and meetings of the Christian Endeavor Society. But during the warm weather, Sundays also meant visits to their cousins in the country, where the long summer evenings were spent sipping lemonade and listening to their great-grandmother retelling stories about their ancestors—the stern New England Puritans, the stalwart immigrants, and the brave pioneer men and women who helped settle Pennsylvania and the mountains of Appalachia.

The Grahams, strict Presbyterians, frowned on worldly pleasures, including dancing. They considered dance lessons an amusement that might divert their daughters from more important pursuits, such as their schoolwork. But they were surprisingly open-minded about other things. They allowed Lizzie Prendergast, who was Catholic, to take Martha to Mass. Martha loved the theatrical pageantry of the church's rites and was enchanted by the colorful rituals and regal mystery of the ceremonies. The memories of the splendors she witnessed as a child stayed with her and influenced her years later when she staged performances for her own dance company. The Grahams also did not mind when the high-spirited Lizzie, who loved attending the theater, delighted her young charges with colorful stories about her evenings there.

Lizzie brought a sense of make-believe and fantasy into the girls' lives. She would help Martha, Mary, and Geordie turn their nursery into a miniature theater, where they would build cities out of wooden blocks and act out elaborate stories and plays, dressed up in their mother's gowns and jewelry. Once, in an attempt to make their theater set more realistic, Martha lit a match in the dollhouse fireplace and accidentally started a fire in the playroom.

George Graham was an important figure in his daughter's life. At bedtime he would often recite exciting tales from the Greek myths, filling Martha's imagination with what she would later call fantastic "word paintings" of the heroic gods and goddesses, kings, queens, and warriors. These stories, Martha said, "fed her imagination" and made her shiver "with wonder and fright."

As the oldest sister, Martha

Martha with her younger sister Mary and their nanny, Lizzie Prendergast (c. 1900)

was sometimes given permission to sit beside her father in the family's horse-drawn buggy, keeping him company as he made his rounds to visit patients. She was also allowed to spend time in her father's book-lined office. Martha loved to read—her favorite book was the dictionary. As a special treat one day, Dr. Graham let her look at a drop of water through his microscope. Amazed to discover the tiny organisms that a moment before had been invisible to her, she realized that one sometimes has to look beneath the surface to discover something's true nature.

When Martha was only four or five years old, her father taught her another lesson—one he had learned from his patients. It was a lesson that would stay with her forever, and she would later rely on it when she began to choreograph and create her own movements and dances. One day, Dr. Graham caught Martha telling a fib. He warned her never to lie to him again. He said he would always know if she was telling the truth just by watching how she moved and held her body and hands. If one knew what to look for, he said, there were clues that would always give liars away. Their poses and gestures—a twitch of the eyelid, a slightly awkward stance, or tilt of the head—would always reveal their true feelings and thoughts. "Movement never lies," he told Martha. This, Martha later said, was her first dance lesson.

In 1908, when Martha was fourteen, the Graham family decided to move to Santa Barbara, on California's Pacific coast. They thought the clean air and bright sunshine would help Mary's chronic asthma. Santa Barbara was markedly different from the dark, grimy place where Martha had grown up, and she would later call her years in California "a time of light, freedom, and curiosity."

Santa Barbara was a city of balmy sea breezes, dazzling azure skies, and brightly colored gardens. The landscape was decorated with sweet-smelling flowers, as well as fragrant citrus orchards and groves of ancient, twisted olive trees. Instead of smoky steel mills, the city had a beautiful old Spanish mission tended by silent, brown-robed Franciscan monks. Santa Barbara not only looked and smelled different from Allegheny; it had a different sound, too. The shrill factory whistles and harsh clank of machinery were replaced by the soft peal of the mission bells and the constant murmur of the Pacific surf. In addition, many of the people of Santa Barbara did not look like the descendants of New England pioneers who lived in Allegheny. In Santa Barbara there was a mix of cultures. The city had been founded and settled by the Spanish in the eighteenth century, so many residents were of Hispanic descent. Others were descendants of the Chinese workers who had been brought to California in the nineteenth century to build the railroads.

Martha was an excellent student. She was imaginative and loved words and language. She enjoyed taking part in school plays and was editor of the school literary magazine. Her teachers thought she might become a writer. Martha was also a fine seamstress and could design, cut, and sew her own clothes. Dr. Graham's mother had attended Vassar College, and Martha's parents valued higher education. They wanted their daughters to get college degrees, although they were not expected to have careers after college but to get married and have children. Martha, always a rebel, had another idea. Ever since she was a little girl, she had loved being in front of an audience, even if it was only made up of her sisters and Lizzie. Martha decided that she would have a career in the theater. "I always loved an audience," she would later say, "from the time I was born."

Although Santa Barbara was a beautiful city, in 1911 it was not a center of culture or art. It did not have a professional theater or a symphony orchestra; traveling companies did not visit. There were few opportunities to see any kind of live theatrical performance.

Then one day, while Martha was out walking with her parents a month before her seventeenth birthday, a poster caught her eye. It announced the Los Angeles appearance of American dancer-choreographer Ruth St. Denis (1878–1968), who had been thrilling audiences with a new kind of dramatic dancing. Martha was spellbound by the portrait on the poster, and she called out to her parents, who had strolled on ahead. To Martha, St. Denis looked like a storybook apparition—beautiful and mysterious. She seemed like a goddess in her richly jeweled Indian-style silk dress and glittering crown. Martha wanted to look just like her.

Dr. Graham still disapproved of dance lessons, but he agreed to take his strong-willed daughter to Los Angeles, one hundred miles away, to attend her first professional dance concert, the

Ruth St. Denis as the Hindu goddess Radha (c. 1911). It was this image, on a poster announcing a dance concert, that so captivated the teenage Martha Graham.

Ruth St. Denis recital. Watching St. Denis perform that day changed Martha's life. As soon as the curtains parted, she knew where her future lay. "From that moment on, my fate was sealed," she later recalled. "I couldn't wait to learn to dance as the goddess did." Although Martha had never even taken a single lesson, she knew she was going to be a dancer.

Martha Graham at the time of her high school graduation (1913)

Graham was a headstrong young woman with an independent spirit. Her parents could never say no to her. After her graduation from high school, she persuaded them to let her live alone in Los Angeles, something few girls of her age or background were allowed to do. There she prepared for her new career by enrolling in an experimental liberal arts college, the Cumnock School of Expression, where she would study dramatics and practical theatrical arts such as lighting and costume design.

In 1914, George Graham, Martha's beloved father, died. His death left the family financially insecure, but there was enough money for Martha to continue her studies at the Cumnock School. She graduated in 1916. The young woman now felt ready to take the final step necessary to fulfill her dream of becoming a dancer. At twenty-two, she was rather old to begin her dance training, but Graham was undaunted. She had heard that Ruth St. Denis and her husband, Ted Shawn (1891–1972), a former divinity student turned dancer, had recently opened an academy of "dancing and related arts" in Los Angeles. Graham applied to the Denishawn School and was accepted.

CHAPTER TWO

With Denishawn

◆

In America during the early years of the twentieth century, most young women, even educated ones like Martha Graham, did not have careers outside the home. Nursing and teaching were among the few jobs that respectable women might hold. Dancing was not a highly regarded profession in the United States. Although classical ballet was considered a serious art form in Europe, there were no classical ballet companies in America. Productions called ballets were gaudy extravaganzas, really more like circuses. For the most part, professional dancers were either scantily clad, high-kicking chorus girls who entertained in burlesque shows or performers in vaudeville acts who specialized in acrobatics, tap, soft shoe, or clog dancing.

Ruth St. Denis, however, was changing the way Americans thought about dance and professional dancers. She appeared on stage barefoot, in colorful native dress. To Western-style music, she performed solo numbers based on ethnic and religious dances from India, China, Japan, Spain, and the Middle East. She used elaborate scenery and wore beautifully ornamented, sometimes revealing, costumes. She would let her prematurely white hair float around her head like a cloud. At other times St. Denis wore exotic wigs and elaborate headdresses. She manipulated veils and scarves so that the fabric seemed alive and part of her body. Miss Ruth, as everyone called her, was graceful, her movements flowing, her body and arms all curves and ripples. In one of her most famous solos, *The Incense,* her body seemed to be made of wafting smoke. In *The Cobra,* her arms became snakes, the rings on her fingers the reptile's glowing eyes. Her dancing was spiritual, but to audiences who thought that even a glimpse of a woman's ankle or an unclothed arm was improper, it was also daring and sexy.

St. Denis's real name was the more American-sounding Ruth Dennis. She had been born on a farm near Newark, New Jersey, and had started her performing career in vaudeville. She knew dancing could be entertainment, but she also felt that it should be treated seriously, an art with high ideals and high standards.

St. Denis and Ted Shawn had a vision that encompassed many different styles and types of dance. The curriculum at the Denishawn School included the basics of classical ballet—although practiced in bare feet rather than toe shoes—as well as classes in character dance and ethnic dance. There were also lessons in "musical visualization," which consisted of dancing to the music of classical composers such as Frédéric Chopin, Johannes Brahms, and Peter Ilyich Tchaikovsky. Even yoga and meditation were part of their program. Courses were given in art, philosophy, music appreciation, and dramatic gesture. There were piano lessons and instruction in lighting, makeup, costume design, even how to pose for publicity photographs. Students were encouraged to read and to go to art galleries and concerts. They were expected to work long and hard. To become professional dancers, they had to be totally dedicated.

This was a revolutionary approach to teaching dance. The school was the first and only one in the United States to have such a total educational program. And unlike the dance academies of Europe, it did not receive any funds from the government. Tuitions helped, but in order to pay the bills, St. Denis, Shawn, and the Denishawn Company of students and professionals had to give public performances. They appeared on vaudeville stages, in silent films, in elaborately staged theatricals of Native American and Hindu dance, and in lavish productions such as their immensely popular *Dance Pageant of Egypt, Greece, and Italy*. Between 1914 and 1931, they made thirteen cross-country tours, bringing serious dance to big cities and small towns throughout the United States. The Denishawn name became synonymous with art and good taste; it was not thought improper for young women and men from respectable families to study at their school in Los Angeles or in the satellite schools they established in other cities.

Martha Graham began her studies at the Denishawn School in the summer of 1916. Like the other older students, she lived at

Ruth St. Denis and Ted Shawn (on rock) with students on the grounds of the Denishawn School (1917). Martha Graham, head bent, is seated on the lower right.

the school, which was located on a beautiful hillside estate above Los Angeles. The Spanish-style mansion was surrounded by fragrant rose arbors, leafy gray eucalyptus trees, and clipped, green lawns on which pet peacocks were allowed to roam. St. Denis thought it was important to be close to nature, and classes were often held in outdoor studios, shaded from the sun by billowing white sheets.

Graham was older than most of the other students. She was a bit overweight and was quiet, awkward, and shy, her face often set in a tight-lipped expression. St. Denis thought her unattractive and "hopeless," and Shawn also thought at first that she lacked the talent necessary to become a dancer. But he soon changed his mind. He realized that Graham's intense desire to dance, her commitment to learn, and her aptitude for acting were more important than her appearance or her late start in training. He encouraged her. So did Louis Horst (1884–1964), the musical director of Denishawn. Although ten years older than the aspiring dancer, he became a close friend and companion and for much of her career was her major musical influence. Only St. Denis remained unimpressed. But Graham was undeterred by the rejection of the "goddess" she worshipped. Although at first she was not allowed to participate, she was permitted to observe classes for the advanced students, where they were taught the dances they would perform on stage. In class, Graham watched intently. A fast learner, she memorized everything. She also spent many nights, alone and in secret, practicing in a darkened studio. Sometimes she would work until dawn, perfecting what she had observed in class. Her hard work and determination began to pay off. By the end of Graham's first year, St. Denis was using her in class to demonstrate basic steps and exercises. Soon she was allowed to teach (at first just to the youngest students, the three- and four-year-olds). Even though she was also now appearing in Denishawn productions as a walk-on or in the chorus, Graham was still not considered for any solo dancing roles.

Graham had matured into a striking young woman with high cheekbones and large blazing eyes. Shawn called her a "beautiful but untamed little black panther." One day, the dancer scheduled to perform the popular solo *Serenata Morisca,* a Moorish-style dance, fell ill. Shawn thought Graham looked right for the role, but since he had not taught her the steps, he didn't think she knew the choreography. Graham insisted that she did and proceeded to amaze everyone with a completely professional rendition of the dance. She was now finally allowed to perform solo numbers on stage. She was also a huge success dancing with Shawn in his elaborate dance-drama, *Xochitl,* about a young girl who becomes empress of the Toltec Indians. Graham's teaching duties also increased.

Martha Graham in *Serenata Morisca* (1921)

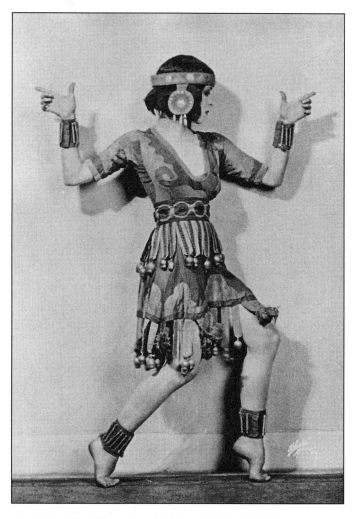

Martha Graham as Xochitl
(1921)

In 1917, America entered World War I (1914–1918). Ted Shawn, who conducted most of the classes at Denishawn, enlisted in the Army. St. Denis, who was always the first to admit that she was not a very good teacher, was spending much of her time touring—performing and helping the war effort by selling Liberty Bonds. As a result, dependable, responsible Graham became the school's chief instructor. Shawn had also been the company's business manager, since St. Denis never concerned herself with such everyday matters as running a dance company. So Graham, despite her lack of actual managerial experience, became the junior director and manager of the Denishawn touring troupe as well. She was put in charge of the group's transportation, hotels, paychecks, costumes, and for making sure that the dancers were on time for each day's three or four performances. She was using her quick wits to learn how to run and manage a dance company.

Now a teacher and manager as well as a professional dancer, Graham was kept busy. But she also felt the need to create her own work, to develop an individual way of expressing the emotions she felt inside her. She realized that the only way to accomplish this was to leave Denishawn.

In 1923, Graham received an offer to appear in the *Greenwich Village Follies,* a popular New York City comedy and musical revue. Hired as a soloist, she was expected to perform well-known pieces such as *Serenata Morisca,* but she could also devise her own dances, as long as they were exotic, like those of Denishawn, and included elaborate costumes and scenery. Graham was soon a star of the *Follies,* but after two years she realized that dance was too serious, too important, for her to remain on the vaudeville stage. Although she had fame, fans, and security (her $350-a-week salary was enormous for the time), she decided to leave the *Follies* and strike out on her own. "I am going to the top. Nothing is going to stop me and I shall do it alone," she said.

Graham's eagerness to be independent and free reflected the postwar atmosphere around her. World War I had been a cruel political conflict that had devastated the European countryside and changed international borders. Its violence brought about a break-down in the old cultural, social, and moral values, which in turn led to changes in the way people behaved. In the United States, the 1920s were called the Roaring Twenties. It was a period of eco-nomic prosperity and dynamism—America was a country on the go. For many women, it was a decade of cultural revolution and political emancipation as well, as they threw off the Victorian restraints left over from the nineteenth century. They were cutting their long hair into "bobs" and casting off their stiff whalebone corsets and long hobble skirts in favor of revealing knee-length flapper dresses. More and more women were working outside of the home, and in 1920, they had won the right to vote. There was a new sense of freedom, frankness, and self-expression, especially in the arts, and Martha Graham wanted to be a part of it.

CHAPTER THREE
A New Language of Dance

◆

Without her salary from the *Follies,* Graham's immediate problem was to support herself while she began her long journey of discovery. She opened a small dance studio in Greenwich Village, the bohemian Manhattan neighborhood known as a center of avant-garde artistic, theatrical, and literary life. She and Louis Horst, who had also recently left Denishawn, got jobs at the Neighborhood Playhouse, where she taught aspiring actors how to move on stage. One of her earliest students was the soon-to-be-famous movie star Bette Davis, who got her first job after Graham taught her how to fall down a flight of stairs without injury.

Graham also commuted two days a week to Rochester, New York, more than 250 miles away, where she was codirector of the Eastman School of Music's dance department. There she had the opportunity to choreograph works on students and to begin developing her own techniques and style. Her first "company" was comprised of three young women from her Eastman classes, the first of many dancers who would become devoted Graham students and followers.

On April 18, 1926, at the Forty-eighth Street Theater in New York City, Martha Graham presented her first independent performance. She was thirty-two years old. Unlike other dancers just starting out on their own, Graham was not content to give her recital in the small, cramped quarters of a church basement or a union hall. Like St. Denis, she wanted to elevate her kind of dancing in the public's eye. So with borrowed money, she rented the stage of a legitimate Broadway theater. She created her own lighting effects and designed and sewed all the costumes. Louis Horst accompanied her on the piano. That night there was a late spring snowstorm, but the theater was filled. Graham said the people came because she "was such a curiosity — a woman who could do her own work."

All of the eighteen solos and trios she presented showed the influence of her Denishawn training. They were soft, romantic, graceful, and mysterious. They had such names as *Three Gopi Maidens, Clair de Lune, Maid with the Flaxen Hair,* and *A Florentine Madonna.*

Graham was not content, however, to go on imitating St. Denis. Nor did she see her future lying in classical ballet. She wanted to create a uniquely American way of moving. She had always been an independent spirit, and now she wanted her own artistic identity.

She did not want to make dances for only others to dance, as most ballet choreographers did. She wanted to perform dances that she had created for her own body. She was rebelling against the artificiality of traditional ballet as well as the exotic pageantry of Denishawn and St. Denis's sometimes inaccurate interpretations of ethnic dancing. Although she had studied ballet technique at Denishawn, Graham didn't think ballet steps and movements could express deep feelings; ballet's vocabulary didn't go far enough for her. She wanted to communicate human experiences and emotions that had never before been explored in dance.

As a young girl and teenager, Graham had been an avid reader. She knew firsthand the magic that language — written and spoken — could evoke. Now she was going to invent her own language, not one made up of words but of steps and gestures. She would speak through her dancing. As she would do throughout her entire career, Graham began to use her classes as an experimental laboratory in which she developed her new language of dance, trying out the movements that would become the trademarks of her style.

Graham later described her method in her early classes:

> [I decided I wouldn't] teach anything I knew. I was through with character dancing. I wanted to begin, not with characters, or ideas, but with movement. So I started with the simplest — walking, running, skipping, leaping. By correcting what looked false, I soon began creating. I wanted sig-

nificant movement. I did not want it to be beautiful or fluid. I wanted it to be [filled] with inner meaning, with excitement and surge.

The central aspect of Graham's emerging technique was something basic and natural, something everyone does in order to live—breathing. Graham was interested in what happens to the body when one breathes, especially when experiencing a deep emotion such as grief (a sob), fear (a gasp), relief (a sigh), or joy (a laugh). She developed an exaggeration of the normal breathing process, which she called contraction and release. Contraction (exhaling) and release (inhaling) were the foundation of all her dance movements. The flow of energy and motion created by a contraction—the action of expelling a breath while tightening and drawing in the lower abdominal muscles—starts in the center of the body, then travels outward to the arms, legs, and head, much the way a pebble, when thrown into water, splashes, then sends out widening ripples along the surface. Graham wanted the entire process to be powerful and visible.

Building on the energy flow and power of the contraction and release, Graham developed, over the years, a number of demanding falls. In these falls, a dancer contracts, or tightens, her torso and knees as she sinks to the ground, giving in to the force of gravity. She then uses the momentum of the fall to rise again, just as a cyclist can coast down a hill and up the other side without pedaling. Graham felt the only reason to do a fall was to rise again. To her, dance should be seamless, a continuous unfolding of movement.

Graham invented many types of long, slow backward falls that were compared to "a dissolving, a melting" to the ground. She described them as letting "a gentle waterfall flow down the body." Graham also devised a sitting position from which the dancer could rise to a standing position on a single count. She would choreograph series of these continuous rises and falls across the stage.

Graham created radically different dance movements that had never been done before. She conceived of spiral twists of the body that one student said resembled "a snake dancing on its tail," and she developed new off-balance positions, in which the dancers leaned backward while on deeply bent knees. She had her dancers skim across the floor with tiny sideways steps, do spins on their knees, or turns in which they tilted their upper bodies close to the ground. Graham could raise her left leg up to the side at a 180-degree angle, and she had her dancers extend their legs as high as possible.

Graham did not want her dances to look like classical ballets, where the effort behind the movements was never to be shown. Effort, to Graham, meant life. Her dancers did not have to defy gravity. She wasn't interested in pretty fairy tales about sleeping princesses or airborne sylphs. In her opinion, dance should speak to people about the times in which they lived, tell them something about their problems and those of their society, and reveal their

Graham relaxing with Louis Horst and her pets (mid-1930s)

deepest emotions. It should make people think. Dance should be a truthful "graph of the heart" and a "landscape of the soul." As she said, she wanted to dance "the reason why."

Meanwhile, Louis Horst was introducing Graham to the music of contemporary American and European composers such as Paul Hindemith, Samuel Barber, Arnold Schoenberg, and Gian Carlo Menotti. He made her realize that nineteenth-century music was not the only music that could be danced to. And for most of her career Graham would, whenever possible, use original commissioned scores to accompany her work.

Like the avant-garde painters, sculptors, architects, and musicians of the day, Graham wanted to simplify and streamline her work. She stripped away fancy trimmings and unnecessary gestures, such as elaborate costumes and fluttering willowy arms. She felt a kinship to expressionist artist Wassily Kandinsky and was particularly drawn to his striking blue canvas with a red slash across it. Graham felt she could evoke in her dance the same impact that painting had had on her. She said, "I will make a dance like that," a dance that would defy the traditional way of doing things. Like the expressionists she admired, Graham was interested in creating works that would induce strong emotional reactions in her audience. Later, in a newspaper interview, she compared her work to "painting with movement," because both have "color," "continuance of line," "shock," and "vibrancy."

CHAPTER FOUR

The Group

◆

It was not always easy for Graham to translate what she felt into dance. The act of creating can often be long, painstaking, and frustrating. She would then turn to her trusted friend Louis Horst, who would calm her down by playing the lilting ragtime tunes of African-American composer Scott Joplin on the piano.

Despite the frustrations, Graham choreographed an astonishing fifty-eight works between 1926 and 1929. There were short solos for herself, including pieces of social commentary such as *Immigrant* (1928), the antiwar *Poems of 1917* (1928), and *Revolt* (1927), a rebellious piece about brutality and injustice, probably the first dance of protest performed in the United States. There were also larger works for an expanded company of female dancers, called the Group, though Graham was still featured as the central dancer. The twelve women in the Group didn't look anything like light and airy ballerinas. They were strong and powerful. They never smiled on stage. They were all devoted to Graham and what she was trying to do. Like Ruth St. Denis, Graham seemed to have a magical, almost religious aura around her that attracted disciples. The members of her troupe certainly weren't there for the money or the recognition, since there weren't many concert dates. They were paid only for performances and even then it was a token ten dollars. Rehearsals were held at dawn or late at night because all the dancers had day jobs—as sales clerks, waitresses, or secretaries—to make ends meet. And Graham often required months of rehearsals for a single night's performance.

Martha Graham and the Group in the early 1930s; the painting is by Paul Meltsner.

Not only did members of the Group not look like dainty ballerinas; they didn't move like ballerinas either. Their movements were sharp, short, and sometimes appeared broken or unfinished. The dancers strode purposefully across the floor, arms swinging. They ran exuberantly; they skipped and leapt. The ground was as important as the air through which they moved. Graham told her dancers "to grab the floor" with their bare feet, to feel the weight of their bodies against it. Instead of opening classes standing at the barre, Graham would begin with the dancers seated on the floor, doing warm-up exercises to help them achieve proper body alignment and to stretch and strengthen their thighs, backs, and torsos. Graham believed that the torso was the source of a dancer's energy and that the spine was "the tree of life."

At the same time, Graham was also experimenting with costumes and makeup. She designed severe tube-shaped dresses of

Graham in her "period of the long woolens" (1933)

Photograph by Soichi Sunami

wool jersey or other stretchy fabrics. Later she would jokingly refer to the late 1920s and early 1930s as her "period of the long woolens." The dresses she designed were ankle- or floor-length and unornamented. They sculpted the body and moved with it. Graham had learned the importance of costumes from Ruth St. Denis — how they could become an actual part of the choreography. Throughout her career, Graham was a stickler about costumes. She wanted them to look good whether the dancer was moving or standing still. She was notorious for making last-minute changes. Her dancers sometimes spent the entire night before a concert resewing costumes that Graham had ripped apart at the dress rehearsal. When there wasn't enough time to finish resewing, they went on stage with their costumes safety-pinned together.

The members of the Group used white makeup so that their faces would look like masks. They imitated Graham's slash of bright red lipstick and pulled their hair straight back into a tight knot as she did. Unkind critics called her grim-faced dancers "Graham Crackers."

During this period, the influential New York newspapers instituted a new department: dance criticism. Up until then, dance performances had been reviewed by the music critics. Sometimes even sports reporters had been sent to cover dance recitals. These new dance critics were noticing Graham's work. It was during this time that people began calling the kind of dances Martha Graham and others were creating "modern dance." But Graham never liked

Graham (in white) and the Group in *Heretic* (1929)

that term. She called her work "contemporary dance" and referred to her pieces as ballets.

In 1929, Graham wrote to a friend, "Life today is nervous, sharp, and zig zag. It often ends in mid air." That also described the dances she made during this period. *Heretic* (1929), which Graham created in one night, is a dance about bigotry, outsiders, and rebels. It is considered her first major work. *Heretic*'s central image is a lone woman dressed in white (Graham) pitted against a double row of stony-faced women in long black dresses, who always move in unison and keep blocking her way. This was a dance that wasn't solely meant to entertain. It was disturbing; it irritated the audience and made them think. The steps were not pretty, the gestures were all angles and straight lines, and the formations were starkly geometric. What's more, the movements did not flow smoothly into one another. They were tense and forceful; the dancers slammed their bare feet into the floor with a driving crash. In contrast to the harsh movements, the music was a simple, lilting Breton folk song, repeated seven times.

Eight months later, on January 8, 1930, Graham performed a startling solo, *Lamentation,* "a dance of sorrows." Throughout the piece, she sat on a low bench, a mummylike figure. Her body was completely covered and hidden by a hooded tube of unadorned jersey in dark lavender, a color sometimes associated with mourning. Only her face, hands, and bare feet were visible. It was a costume she said, that showed "the ability to stretch inside your skin."

Photograph by Soichi Sunami

Graham in *Lamentation* (1930)

As Zoltán Kodály's somber music started, Graham began to move within the material, straining against it, convulsively twisting and swaying from side to side, up and down. Most of the time, her feet did not leave the floor. There were none of the steps, jumps, or movements usually associated with dance. Graham leaned off-balance, tensed, stretched, and rocked back and forth, a writhing, sculpted figure of changing shapes and angles. With no reference to a specific tragedy, she portrayed the feelings of deepest anguish and unbearable loss through her body alone. "Martha Graham does not depict grief; she *is* grief," said one reviewer. After a performance of *Lamentation,* a woman came backstage to thank Graham for the ballet. She said that until she saw the dance, she had been unable to mourn or cry for her young child who had died several months before.

In the summer of 1930, Graham and Louis Horst took a vacation to the Southwest. They were captivated by the landscape—the harsh desert, the luminous sunlight, the shadow-tinged mountains that rose majestically into the clear blue sky. They were also captivated by the Native Americans of the region, whose culture, over the centuries, had been influenced by Spanish-Mexican Catholicism. Graham and Horst visited many of the area's one-room adobe churches, decorated with carved and painted images of Christ on the cross, called *santos,* and with wooden, doll-like statues of the Virgin Mary dressed in white. They also attended stately yet simple religious ceremonies and public processionals, whose

Graham (center, in white) and the Group in *Primitive Mysteries* (1931)

rituals reminded Graham of the Masses she had attended with Lizzie Prendergast back in Santa Barbara.

When she returned to New York, Graham began work on a new dance inspired by what she had seen in New Mexico. At the same time, Horst was composing the score for flute, oboe, and piano, music that sounded faintly like Native American melodies. *Primitive Mysteries,* a dance for a soloist (Graham) dressed in white and twelve women (the Group), dressed in deep blue, premiered on February 2, 1931.

Primitive Mysteries was influenced by Catholic-Indian ceremonial rituals that honored the Virgin Mary; its three sections are entitled Hymn to the Virgin, Crucifixus, and Hosanna. But it is also a work about religious feelings in general. In later years Graham described it as "a celebration of the coming of age of a young girl." Each of the ballet's three sections opens and closes with a solemn, silent procession, where every footstep can be heard. The women in blue appear to worship the girl in white, glorifying her purity. At one point their hands form a halo around her head, their fingers spread like rays of light. They pray with her, grieve with her, rejoice with her. Her body moves in a simple, gentle, uncluttered way, while in contrast, the group's gestures are angular and powerful.

The cheering audience gave *Primitive Mysteries* thirty-two curtain calls. The dance critics called it "a masterpiece, probably the finest single composition ever produced in America." Martha Graham's stage was about to expand.

CHAPTER FIVE

Recognition

◆

The critics were not the only ones noticing Martha Graham's talents as a dancer, choreographer, and teacher. Students from all over the country were coming to her classes, and in January of 1932, Graham and the Group were asked to perform in the opening program at New York's Radio City Music Hall. Unfortunately, her work wasn't appropriate for that cavernous 6,200-seat theater, and the dancers were described by *The New Yorker* magazine as looking like mice scampering across the huge stage.

Two months later, Graham received a John Guggenheim Memorial Fellowship, the first ever awarded to a dancer. Friends suggested that she use the grant money to go to Germany and work with Mary Wigman, a teacher, choreographer, and dancer pioneering modern dance in Europe. But Graham decided to stay closer to home. That summer she went to Mexico to visit several recently excavated archeological sites. She felt that by studying the

Graham atop the Pyramid of
the Sun, Mexico (1932)

ancient American civilizations of the Mayas and Aztecs, she could gain "the ability to identify . . . with a culture that wasn't mine." In the Yucatán she climbed to the top of the sacred Pyramid of the Sun, where she was enthralled "by the wind, and the sun, the height of [this] very hallowed place." Her visit to Mexico fired her imagination and reinforced her love for Native American peoples and their customs.

Despite the increased recognition, Graham still had her detractors. The worlds of classical ballet and modern dance continued to eye each other uneasily. The great Russian ballet dancer-choreographer Michel Fokine had contributed some revolutionary ideas to classical dance earlier in the century. He had introduced reforms and a new sense of freedom into ballet music, costumes, and movement. Sometimes he even had his ballerinas dance in bare feet. But he described Martha Graham and her work as "Ugly girl makes ugly movements on stage while ugly mother tells ugly brother to make ugly sounds on drum." One drama critic, dismayed at the sharp angles and geometric shapes in Graham's works, suggested that if she ever gave birth, it would be to a cube.

The 1930s were a difficult time for all artists. It was the Great Depression (1930–1939), a period of social, economic, and political unrest, not only in the United States but around the world as well. In America, 30 percent of the population was out of work. Breadlines and soup kitchens helped feed the unemployed. Fewer and fewer people could afford tickets to cultural events, but Graham tried to give concerts whenever she could. Money was always a problem. She had to live frugally. Her studio became her home. Her furnishings consisted of a table, some chairs, a cot, a chest of drawers, a record player, and in one corner, Louis Horst's baby grand piano.

In the summer of 1934, Graham was one of several contemporary dancers and choreographers asked to participate in a wholly new kind of dance program at Bennington College, in Vermont. Bennington, a progressive liberal arts college for women, had been founded two years before. The school's dance department was headed by Martha Hill, a former member of Graham's Group. It was her idea to stage a Festival of Dance each summer, where physical education teachers (who were responsible for teaching dance in high schools and colleges) as well as aspiring and professional dancers would have the opportunity to work with the best choreographers and stage designers. Hill wanted the most important names in modern dance to be associated with her Festival. She invited the so-called "Big Four": Graham, Doris Humphrey (1895–1958), Charles Weidman (1901–1975), and Hanya Holm (1893–1992), a noted German dancer-choreographer who had recently settled in the United States. Louis Horst was asked to teach musical composition for dance. They were all provided with studios, workshops, and theater space, rent free.

This innovative program, which continued until the early 1940s, was a success from the start. The first year, one hundred women, ranging in age from fifteen to forty-nine, enrolled. These students then helped spread an interest in modern dance across the country. During the 1930s many young people were drawn to modern dance because its freedom of movement gave them a new and almost unlimited way to express themselves.

During the late 1920s and early 1930s, most of Graham's dances had as their theme the plight of the outsider, the outcast, or the rebel pitted against the will of the majority. Other works mirrored the social unrest of the time. Graham's style reflected the struggles, tensions, and frustrations of the period but also those experiences felt by an artist as individualistic as she was.

By the middle of the decade, however, things were beginning to change, both for Graham and for the country. Through her classes, performances, and her work with Bennington students, more and more people were coming to understand and appreciate her dances. She was no longer a total outsider. Graham was ready to explore new ways in which dance could speak to people about their time. America was turning a corner, too. President Franklin D. Roosevelt's New Deal policies were beginning to instill a sense of public confidence that although it would take some time, the country might be able to pull through the Depression.

It was during this period that Graham's style began to change. It became less angular, less grim. She began to use decor and stage settings for the first time. As she had done with costumes, she would bring innovations to set decoration that would eventually be acclaimed and adapted throughout the entire theatrical world. The themes of her ballets were also changing dramatically. Over the next few years she would create some of her most enduring and popular works.

In 1936, Graham told a newspaper interviewer, "No artist is ahead of his time. He *is* his time." The Depression was a period of great patriotism in all the arts, but Graham was the first to reflect this love of one's country in dance. Graham saw that despite the hard times, the American people had a unique and enduring energy and vitality, a positive force that had been evident from the country's earliest days. She knew she could express this energy in her work. During times of economic and political troubles, people need to see and hear good things about their lives. Americans needed to believe that there was some hope for their future. Graham would help inspire that hope by showing American audiences something about their past. Remembering the stories that her great-grandmother had told about her brave pioneer ancestors,

Graham began to turn her attention to dances that reflected American themes and the country's historical heritage.

Frontier, just six and a half minutes long, premiered on April 28, 1935; it would become one of Graham's most celebrated solos. The piece was subtitled "An American Perspective of the Plains," and in its movements, setting, costume, and music (composed by Louis Horst), it evoked the freedom, spirit, and confidence of a people who had carved a nation out of a wilderness. This was the first work in which Graham did not dance on a bare stage; the added set designs were the result of her first collaboration with sculptor Isamu Noguchi. Their innovative artistic partnership would last fifty-three years.

Isamu Noguchi (1904–1988) was born in Los Angeles; his mother was an American writer, his father a Japanese poet. The family soon moved to Yokohama, Japan, but Noguchi returned to

Artist Isamu Noguchi. His collaboration with Martha Graham, which lasted more than fifty years, began in 1935 with *Frontier.*

Martha Graham in *Frontier* (1935)

the United States as a teenager to study art. Graham had met him in the late 1920s, when his sister had been a member of the Group.

The set for *Frontier* was Noguchi's first. It is simple yet powerful: two parallel bars of raw wood form a fence placed against a black curtain. From the floor behind the fence rails, two thick white ropes stretch diagonally off into the wings, forming a giant V that opens toward the audience. This V creates the illusion of unlimited space, like the vast uncharted openness of a young America. The set looks nothing like the two-dimensional painted backdrops or flats that had usually been used in dance and theatrical performances. It is three-dimensional, like a piece of sculpture. The fence itself became part of the choreography. Graham was seen leaning against it as the piece opens. She stood with one foot planted firmly on it; she rested against it as she surveyed the stage. She kept leaving it, then returning to it. Graham's choreography, though based on simple steps, was freer than in her earlier pieces; she did not dance with a masklike face—she even smiled. In a long, plain brown-and-white dress of rough homespun, she was every courageous, strong, and independent pioneer woman who had ever faced the challenge of taming and settling a new land.

During the next two years, Graham continued to create new solos and group numbers. In 1936, she managed to take her dancers cross-country on the first transcontinental tour ever

By the mid-1930s, Martha Graham was established as one of the leaders of the modern dance movement. Here she poses dramatically for a cover of *Dance* magazine in 1936.

undertaken by a modern American dance troupe. Many reviewers still did not understand her work: "The most perplexing of American dancers . . . [her] programs stir controversy . . . for no one is dispassionate about her," wrote the *Detroit News*. Despite the controversy, in 1937, Graham became the first American dancer to receive an invitation to perform at the White House. The request came from the president's wife, Eleanor Roosevelt.

The news that Graham was an important artist was spreading beyond the United States as well. The year before, she had received an invitation from the government of Nazi Germany to perform at the Olympic Games in Berlin. Such a performance would have given her recognition throughout the world, but she adamantly refused. "I would find it impossible to dance in Germany at the present time," she wrote to Joseph Goebbels, the propaganda minister.

> So many artists whom I respect and admire have been persecuted, have been deprived of the right to work for ridiculous and unsatisfactory reasons, that I should consider it impossible to identify myself, by accepting the invitation, with the regime that has made such things possible.

Many members of the Group were Jewish, the minority most persecuted by the Nazis, and Graham was also worried about their safety. Years later, Graham found out that after receiving her letter of refusal, the Nazis, angered by her response, had put her name on a list of "undesirable" people to be murdered.

CHAPTER SIX

Changes

◆

Instead of going to the Olympics in Berlin, Graham returned to Bennington, Vermont. There, in the summer of 1936, she met a young American ballet dancer named Erick Hawkins. Their meeting would have an important effect on Martha Graham's work and personal life. Hawkins (1909–1994), born in Trinidad, Colorado, was tall and muscular, with a handsome, rugged face. Although he was a member of Ballet Caravan, a small, fledgling company founded by Lincoln Kirstein, the young dancer felt that classical ballet did not offer him all that he was seeking from dance. Kirstein had suggested that Hawkins study with Graham.

Soon, Hawkins was not only attending Graham's classes but, at her invitation, was also teaching her students basic ballet movements. Although Graham generally did not use the vocabulary of classical ballet, she recognized its usefulness in making dancers more flexible, and she had always respected its training methods. "I never wanted to destroy ballet, I only went my own way," she said. "All dance is universal and there are only two types of dance, the good and the bad."

Hawkins was even allowed to watch rehearsals for a major new work—a celebration of American democracy—that Graham was creating. Then, to everyone's surprise and to the dismay of Louis Horst and others, Graham asked Hawkins to join the Group as a principal dancer, the first male in her troupe. He would be the only other designated soloist besides herself. The addition of a male dancer signaled an end to the Group. Several longtime members left, some upset that they had been passed over to be soloists. Over the next few years, four other men would join the troupe.

Erick Hawkins, Doris Humphrey, Charles Weidman, Martha Graham, and Louis Horst at Bennington College (1941)

As Ted Shawn had done for Ruth St. Denis, it wasn't long before Hawkins took on management, fund-raising, and other business duties. He often conducted rehearsals so that Graham could concentrate on more creative matters. Everyone knew that when a red ribbon was tied to the studio door, no one was to enter, because Martha was not to be disturbed. She was making a new dance.

The addition of Hawkins into the troupe gave Graham the opportunity to create her first pas de deux, or male-female duets. These "conversations" between dancers of different sexes provided electricity and a new dramatic tension that had been lacking in her earlier all-female pieces. Graham could now explore emotions between men and women, such as love, hate, and jealousy. And her interpretations of American traditions and history could now include the male experience as well. Graham's choreography seemed to have more warmth, was freer and more lyrical, and for the first time, she used bright colors in her costumes. Her female dancers looked different, too. They were no longer the robust, slow-moving, powerful women of *Heretic.* Sleeker, thinner, smaller, they moved with speed and lightness.

Graham cast Hawkins as the male lead in the new piece, called *American Document,* which premiered at Bennington in the summer of 1938. *American Document* was different from Graham's previous dances. It was the first of several works to combine dance with drama in the form of a spoken narrative. Graham once said, "I have

Graham and Erick Hawkins rehearsing
American Document at Bennington College (1938)

a holy attitude toward books. . . . Words are magical and beautiful."
With *American Document,* her language of dance expanded to
include words.

When Graham took the piece on tour, its popularity made
modern dance acceptable to a broader audience. A dance everyone could understand, it reflected traditional American ideals as
well as the country's new feelings of hope, optimism, and renewal.
America was coming out of the Depression. Factories were
reopening, and more people were working. Although the political
news from Europe was not good because of continuing talk of war,
there was a sense that the country had survived a terrible time

with its values intact. *American Document* also had the contemporary "sex appeal" of the popular entertainments of the day— Hawkins, good-looking and well built, danced part of his role bare-chested.

American Document presented a panorama of American history in the form of a minstrel show, an entertainment popular in the nineteenth century. "Our documents are our legends," said Graham, "our folk tales." So she took the words for the narration from a number of famous texts: the Declaration of Independence, a letter written by Seneca chief Red Jacket, Abraham Lincoln's Gettysburg Address, the fiery sermons of eighteenth-century Massachusetts preacher Jonathan Edwards, the Bible's Song of Solomon, and Walt Whitman's poetry. The dance included an Indian Episode ("Lament for the Land") as well as a Puritan Episode, a duet for Graham and Hawkins. In this pas de deux, the beautiful poetry of the Old Testament love songs was contrasted with the forceful words of the stern New England Puritan. There was also an Episode for the Emancipation Proclamation, which celebrated individual freedom, and one called The Present, showing the country's strength, vitality, and hope. The score, by Ray Green, used familiar folk songs as well as original music.

The popularity of *American Document* meant that Martha Graham was no longer an outsider whose work was sometimes misunderstood and mocked by critics and the general public. She was able to arrange more cross-country tours, bringing her dances to ever widening and appreciative audiences.

CHAPTER SEVEN

A Letter to the World

◆

Erick Hawkins was featured in Graham's next two important works, pieces that also introduced the second male dancer into the troupe. Merce Cunningham, born in 1919 in Centralia, Washington, joined the Group in 1939. His dancing had an airborne quality; he was fast and an excellent jumper. In *El Penitente* (to music by Louis Horst), Graham returned for inspiration to her beloved Southwest and to its blend of Native American and Hispanic culture, which had inspired *Primitive Mysteries* nine years before. The title of the new work refers to the region's Penitente sect, whose members practiced acts of extreme penance to purify themselves of sins. Once again Graham created a dance with a theatrical setting: This time a group of strolling players present scenes from the Bible in an open-air Passion Play.

El Penitente's premiere at Bennington on August 11, 1940, was a great success. That night, another major ballet featuring Graham,

Hawkins, and Cunningham was also performed for the first time. *Letter to the World* was based on an unlikely subject for dance: the life and writings of the shy and retiring nineteenth-century New England poet Emily Dickinson. As the daughter of a doctor who had treated diseases of the mind, it was perhaps natural that Graham would be interested in creating dances that explored not only a character's behavior but also her "inner landscape"— her thoughts, feelings, and motivations. *Letter to the World* was Graham's first attempt to compose a biographical and psychological portrait in dance; before she began the project, she had read everything she could about Dickinson and her poetry.

Emily Dickinson (1830–1886) wrote more than 1,500 short, original gemlike poems that deal symbolically with love, death, and nature. She lived most of her life in Amherst, the small Massachusetts town where she had been born. In her late twenties, she began to withdraw from public view, eventually becoming a recluse in her father's house. Only seven of her poems were published in her lifetime, but after her death, the private and sensitive "Belle of Amherst" was hailed as a major American artist.

Letter to the World (to music by Hunter Johnson) was Graham's most ambitious work to this point. It has acts and scenes, like a play. The decor by Arch Lauterer, a designer Graham had met at Bennington, consists of an airy white latticework garden gate and a shuttered doorway. Like *American Document, Letter to the World* combines dance with the spoken word, the dancing reflecting the narration, which is comprised of Dickinson's poems. The character

Martha Graham in *Letter to the World* (1940)

of Dickinson is portrayed by two women: One Who Dances, who represents the poet's inner, hidden life of creativity, the part of her that gave rise to her poetry, and One Who Speaks, who represents the outer, proper, decorous, dignified Emily Dickinson that the world knew. At the premiere, Graham took the role of the One Who Dances; Jean Erdman was the One Who Speaks.

Although *Letter to the World* is a biographical ballet, it does not tell Dickinson's life story in a chronological way. It uses flashbacks, skipping back and forth in time, and it skips back and forth between the poet's inner and outer lives as well. These narrative techniques—flashbacks and the use of multiple dancers to portray different aspects of one character—were new to dance; Graham would continue to use and develop them in many future works.

At the beginning of the piece, both Emilys greet each other and acknowledge their kinship: "I am nobody! / Who are you? / Are you nobody, too? / Then there's a pair of us." Other characters represent aspects of Dickinson's personality in childhood, adolescence, and young womanhood. Another character, the Ancestress, a stern, yet beautiful woman in somber black dress, who Graham said was modeled after her great-grandmother, represents Dickinson's New England heritage; the Ancestress is a symbol of Puritan tradition and authority. Hawkins was cast as the Lover, and Merce Cunningham as March, the spirit of spring.

The ballet closes with a sweeping, passionate solo for Graham ("This is my letter to the World / That never wrote to Me"), which ends with her sitting on a garden bench, calm, composed, resigned to the choices she has made in her life. Graham's portrayal of Emily Dickinson was a picture of an artist who chose to give up ordinary life in order to follow an inner need to create another world with her poetry. In this portrait, Graham had also composed a letter about herself. She was sending her world a message about her own struggles against convention and what it meant for a woman to sacrifice a personal life to dedicate herself absolutely to her art.

Despite its originality, *Letter to the World* did not receive good reviews after its Bennington premiere. Graham herself wasn't satisfied with the piece because she hadn't really had enough time to work on it. But four months later, in January 1941, when a revised version was presented in New York City, the critics changed their minds. John Martin, the dance critic for the *New York Times,* called it "extraordinarily successful in capturing the flavor of . . . the poet's most radiant lines and making them unimaginably poignant."

With works such as *American Document* and *Letter to the World,* Graham was on her way to establishing what would become known around the world as the "dance-theater" of Martha Graham, a complete theatrical experience in which movement would be combined with music, costumes, sets, and sometimes words or narration, in dances of passionate drama.

The popular theater had been a part of Graham's early professional life with Denishawn and the *Follies.* She now began to realize that even the most independent and serious of artists needs to entertain her audience, at least some of the time, if she wishes to keep them. In 1941, just before the New York premiere of *Letter to the World,* she told an interviewer:

> I'm afraid I used to hit audiences over the head with a sledgehammer because I was so determined that they see and feel what I was trying to do. We must win back our audiences. We have alienated them through grimness of theme and a nontheatrical approach to our dancing. Now that we have left our period of 'long woolens' behind us, we must prove [that our dances] have color, warmth, and entertainment values. We must convince [audiences] that we belong in the American Theater.

Graham's reputation and popularity continued to grow. She was attracting the attention not only of the press but of other celebri-

In her studio, Graham and her group help Helen Keller experience the joy of dance (early 1940s).

ties as well. One frequent visitor to her studio on lower Fifth Avenue was Helen Keller, the popular American author, lecturer, and activist. Blind and deaf since the age of two, this courageous woman had a unique way of enjoying dance. Keller, who perceived the world through her fingers and her acute sense of touch, experienced Graham and her group by feeling the vibrations that the impact of their feet made on the floor. One day, Keller asked Graham to explain jumping. To illustrate this simple movement, Graham placed Keller's hands on Merce Cunningham's waist, keeping them there as he leapt up and down. Soon a look of joy animated Keller's face. Flinging her arms in the air, this woman who lived in a dark and silent universe exuberantly declared, "How like thought. How like the mind it is."

CHAPTER EIGHT

Appalachian Spring

◆

On December 7, 1941, when the Japanese bombed the American naval base at Pearl Harbor, Hawaii, the United States was irretrievably drawn into the conflict that had been engulfing Europe and Asia for several years. The Graham troupe, now renamed Martha Graham and Company, was not, however, directly affected by the United States' entry into World War II (1939–1945). Most of the dancers were women and therefore not subject to the draft, and Erick Hawkins was rejected by the Army for his extreme near-sightedness. Even though the country was mobilizing for war and there were very few concert dates, Graham kept on working, creating her distinctive kind of dance.

In 1943, Graham created *Deaths and Entrances* (to music by Hunter Johnson), another of her unique psychological biographical ballets that presented a dance portrait of characters' inner landscapes. Still a voracious reader, she had been drawn to the works and lives of the mysterious Brontë sisters. Charlotte, Emily, and Anne Brontë were nineteenth-century British writers best known for their passionate and romantic novels, including *Jane Eyre* (Charlotte), *Wuthering Heights* (Emily), and *The Tenant of Wildfell Hall* (Anne). Despite the critical success of their books, their personal lives were not happy. With their ne'er-do-well brother, the sisters lived in poverty in a bleak parsonage on the wild Yorkshire moors. All the Brontës had begun writing as children—it was the inner world of the imagination that enabled the sisters to cope with their hard life. But their writing careers were tragically brief; not one of the sisters lived to be forty. Some people thought *Deaths and Entrances* was really about Graham and her family. Many years later, she told an interviewer: "The work is not a mirror of my life, but speaks to anyone who has a family. It is a modern psychological portrait of women unable to free themselves to follow their heart's desires."

As she had done for *Letter to the World* and would continue to do from then on, Graham read extensively about the subject of the dance she was considering, keeping notebooks filled with thoughts and instructions. She then prepared a detailed scenario, or script—all this before she set foot in the studio to begin choreographing. She explained her method:

> I get the idea going. Then I write it down, I copy out of any book that stimulates me at the time any quotation, and I keep it. And I put down the source. Then when it comes to

the actual work, I keep a complete record of the steps. I just put it down and know what the words mean or what the movements mean and where you go and what you do and maybe an explanation here and there.

For example, directions for one work, taken from her notebooks, begin:

> Scene opens—
> sound—
> light slowly
> woman with long gold hair walks to back and disappears < fades—
>   pales?

A record of the steps might read:

> 1. circular kick
> 2. circular kick
> 3. darts
> 4. bow—hands on knees
>   wide second [position]
> 5. circular kick
> 6. circular kick
> 7. simple bow
> 8. arise with arms up high

When she then began to work with her dancers, she would ask them to approach their parts as an actor would. They should think about the characters they were portraying—not only how those characters might do the steps she gave them but also how they would react in situations not portrayed on stage. The dancers should know their characters so well that they could say what they had eaten for breakfast.

In the 1940s, the government did not have any programs to help subsidize the arts or artists. So despite Graham's growing popularity as a performer and choreographer, she found it difficult to obtain the funds she needed to put her work on stage as often as she would have liked. The salaries she received from teaching her own classes as well as those at the Neighborhood Playhouse weren't enough. She was using more elaborate costumes, sets, and scores, and they all cost money. She had also hired her first lighting director, Jean Rosenthal, who was in the forefront of revolutionizing theatrical lighting. She and Graham would collaborate over the years on many pieces, working to make the lighting a partner of the dancing.

Hawkins, who was the company's fund raiser, discovered that one of Graham's students, Bethsabee de Rothschild, was a member of a wealthy international banking family. Rothschild, who was Jewish, had fled France early in the war. She had settled in New York City and had become one of Graham's most devoted disciples. The five hundred dollars Rothschild gave Graham in 1943 to have the score for *Deaths and Entrances* orchestrated began her twenty-year financial support of the company.

Hawkins was also instrumental in getting Elizabeth Sprague

Coolidge, a wealthy patron of the arts, to commission Graham to create three new works to be premiered at a concert at the Library of Congress in Washington, D.C. One of the new pieces, *Appalachian Spring,* was to be a joyous tribute to America's heritage, specifically to the men and women who, like Graham's forebears, had settled the mountains and valleys of Pennsylvania.

Whereas Graham's earlier work *Frontier* is about pioneers moving into open, uncharted spaces, *Appalachian Spring* (1944) focuses on a frontier that had already been tamed and domesticated and on the settlers who put down roots there. It is a celebration of a simpler past. But in its sense of optimism and hope in the future, it also reflected a contemporary America that had experienced the Great Depression and World War II but could now envision the coming of a better and more prosperous future. "America," Graham said, "is forever peopled with characters who walk with us in the present in a very real way."

Part of the commission included money for Graham to choose composers to write new scores. For *Appalachian Spring*'s music, Graham turned to Aaron Copland (1900–1990), a forty-four-year-old Brooklyn-born composer who several years earlier had been praised for his scores for two ballets with American themes: *Billy the Kid* and *Rodeo.* He accepted the new commission and composed a lush, glowing score with a folk flavor incorporating the traditional Shaker hymn "Simple Gifts." The music perfectly conveyed the freshness of leafy green woods and newly sprouted fields, the peace and quiet of the rural landscape, and the joys and pleasures of friendship and love. Copland called his piece "Ballet for Martha." Years later, he told an interviewer:

> It was her personal manner that inspired the style of the music. Martha is rather prim and restrained, simple yet strong, and her dance style is correspondingly direct. One thinks of those qualities as being especially American and, thus, the character of my score, which quotes only one actual folk tune, but which uses rhythms, harmonies and melodies that suggest an American ambiance.

In 1945, Copland was awarded the Pulitzer Prize in music for his "Ballet for Martha."

For her set designs, Graham once again turned to Isamu Noguchi. He created a simple yet elegant scene, one that was architectural rather than sculptural: a partial, skeletal cross section of a white clapboard house with a peaked roof; a rocking chair on a front porch; a tree stump; a bench; and a section of fence rail, the boundary of the new homestead. He said he wanted the stage to look "empty, yet full at the same time."

Graham worked closely with Copland and Noguchi on *Appalachian Spring,* and their collaboration is considered one of the greatest in the American theater. Graham once explained how she worked with composers. She would give them a detailed scenario, which included quotes and passages from the books she had been

Appalachian Spring (1944): Erick Hawkins (in foreground) as the Husband, Graham (seated) as the Bride, and May O'Donnell (standing) as the Pioneer Woman. Isamu Noguchi's architectural scenery depicts the framework of a clapboard house.

reading that related to the subject, along with notations on where there would be a solo, a duet, or a dance for the entire group. "I never cut a composer's music," she said. "I never cut him down to time. When I get the music, I start to choreograph."

Her collaborations with set designers took a similar form. For example, she would tell Noguchi the theme or story upon which the piece was to be based. He would then ask her if she had any special requirements. How much space did she need for her dancers? Did she need something for them to sit or stand on, or something to hide behind? Sometimes Graham, who liked to work late at night, would telephone him at one A.M. to discuss what she wanted. Next, Noguchi would devise a scale model of the stage for Graham to work with. Since many of her dances were done to commissioned scores, Noguchi often did not hear the music until after his designs were finished.

Appalachian Spring, Graham's last ballet to have such an American theme, was also her most free-spirited. It was an instant and tremendous hit; performances were sold out night after night. A masterpiece that showed Graham's genius for telling stories through dance, this tender and poetic ballet became her most popular work and her company's signature piece.

The original program note succinctly described *Appalachian Spring* as "Spring celebrated by a man and a woman building a house." Dancer and choreographer Agnes de Mille, Graham's longtime friend, described it more fully as:

> a love letter, a dance of hope, budding, fresh, and beautiful.
> . . . The characters were the young bride, the young groom, the older woman who was the advisor and protector, and the preacher, a brimstone frontier evangelist who prophesied doom and hellfire . . . followed and supported by . . . a group of devout young spinsters.

The opening night cast included May O'Donnell as the Pioneer Woman and Merce Cunningham, who would leave the company the following year to form his own modern dance group, as the revivalist Preacher. Graham, then fifty years old, danced the Bride, and Hawkins the Husband. Each character had a solo that revealed his or her personality and emotions: the Pioneer Woman's wisdom and experience; the Preacher's religious authority and spellbinding power; the Husband's solid strength, warmth, and practicality; and the Bride's nervous excitement and joyous rapture. Although Graham had long been acknowledged as a great dramatic actress, this was one role in which she did not have to pretend. She and Hawkins had fallen very much in love.

CHAPTER NINE

Women of Myth and Legend

◆

With the success of *Appalachian Spring,* Graham's reputation and standing in the dance world were secured. The former outsider and rebel was a celebrity. Unlike many celebrities, however, she was protective of her private life. Shy and not fond of speaking about herself in public, Graham didn't like to give interviews or to have her picture taken offstage. She did agree, however, to lecture and teach at colleges and universities, and she was invited to be on the dance faculty of the prestigious Juilliard School of Music, in New York City. Modern dance was gaining wider acceptance and was no longer considered outside the mainstream. Even Broadway shows were adapting the kind of dances that Graham had developed, dances that showed the inner feelings of a character. *Oklahoma!* (1943), one of the longest running and most popular musicals in Broadway history, included a psychological dream ballet choreographed by Agnes de Mille.

Arrangements for the company's tours were taken over by producer Sol Hurok, the country's foremost impresario, known for sponsoring performances of the world's most famous entertainers. With Bethsabee de Rothschild's financial help, Graham no longer had to live as simply as she once had. She could now afford the designer dresses and jewelry she loved, a nicer apartment, antique furniture, a cook and maid, everything that befitted her new status as "high priestess" of modern dance.

Although Graham was now well known and works like *Appalachian Spring* were seen as popular entertainment, she refused to compromise on the seriousness of her art. She would continue to create pieces that audiences would at first consider difficult to understand.

Having looked at America's history and heritage, Graham now turned to stories from Greek mythology and the Bible for her inspiration. She continued her interest in portraying human experiences that hadn't been explored fully in dance. Her new ballets concentrated on exposing intense emotions through dance: fear, hate, tenderness, jealousy, anxiety, greed, love, rage, remorse, grief, self-doubt. These emotions, which are universal, would be experienced in her ballets by legendary women, larger-than-life heroines who come to know themselves.

Her collaborator on most of the ballets in her so-called Greek Cycle was Isamu Noguchi, who designed unusual and striking decor and props. Some of his set designs were strange three-dimensional shapes, abstract sculptural forms that might look like

giant boulders, bones, or wooden beams. His work helped trans-
form the stage into a place of the imagination, a visual depiction of
the inner landscapes, or states of mind, of Graham's characters.
Noguchi thought of his sets as sculptural objects that the dancers
could move through, carry, manipulate, or dance around. Graham
said that his sculptures took her "to images that [she] had never
contemplated before." Noguchi's sets, which served both symbolic
and functional purposes, became a seamless part of Graham's
dances.

Cave of the Heart (1946, to music by Samuel Barber) is a portrait
of evil. Its subject is the power of jealous hatred; it is a dance,

Graham in *Cave of the Heart*
(1946), wearing Isamu
Noguchi's wire "dress"

according to the original program notes, "of possessive and destroying love, a love which feeds upon itself like a serpent heart, and when it is overthrown, is fulfilled only in revenge." It tells the story of the Greek sorceress Medea, who poisoned her rival and killed her own children out of jealousy and revenge over the unfaithfulness of her husband, Jason. In one of the most stunning scenes, Medea, danced with ferocious intensity by Graham, draws a snakelike blood red ribbon out of her mouth, the symbol of all the venomous hatred she has inside her. Medea's headdress is a mass of reptilian coils, snarling snakes of jealousy. Her gold wire dress, designed by Noguchi, is both a costume and a prop; it becomes the cage that eventually imprisons her.

Errand into the Maze (1947, to music by Gian Carlo Menotti) was inspired by the legend of the Minotaur, the monster with the head of a bull and the body of a man, who lived in the Labyrinth, a winding, mazelike cave on the island of Crete. There, the Minotaur devoured the Greek youths and maidens who were sacrificed to him. No one had been able to kill the monster, because no one knew how to find a way back out of the cave.

In the original tale, Ariadne, a Cretan princess, gives Theseus the clue that enables him to escape from the Minotaur: If he unwinds a ball of thread as he descends into the Labyrinth, he will be able to retrace his steps. In Graham's version of the myth, she again brings forward a strong female character. In *Errand into the Maze,* it is Ariadne, not Theseus, who does successful battle with the Minotaur, now called the Creature of Fear. Her journey into the maze represents the journey to face the fears, insecurities, and self-doubts that everyone feels at some point in his or her life. Ariadne's destruction of the monster becomes the conquering of her own fears, something that she can do only when she faces those fears directly.

Graham would eventually do eleven dances inspired by Greek legends, including one of her most acclaimed dramatic roles. She was nearly sixty-five years old when she danced the title character, the wife of King Agamemnon, in *Clytemnestra* (1958, to music by Halim El-Dabh). The first evening-length modern dance work, *Clytemnestra* is an intense dance-drama of love, treachery, and betrayal. Clytemnestra's murder of her husband after he returns home from the Trojan Wars sets off a bloody cycle of revenge, retribution, and death.

Graham's exploration of strong Biblical and religious women resulted in *Judith* (1950, to music by William Schuman) a demanding twenty-five-minute solo about the Old Testament heroine who murdered a tyrant in order to save her people, and *The Triumph of Saint Joan* (1951, to music by Norman Dello Joio), a solo portrait of Joan of Arc.

In the summer of 1948, Martha created a dance that was decidedly different from the dark and dramatic pieces of the previous few years. *Diversion of Angels* (music by Dello Joio) is a lighthearted ode to youth, a lyrical dance about the joys and occasional pains of being in love for the first time. Although several years earlier Graham had finally allowed some dancers in her company to perform roles she had originated, *Diversion of Angels* was the first new work in which Graham did not dance. Perhaps that was why it also became one of a very few of her ballets that she would allow other companies to perform. Shortly after it premiered, Graham and Hawkins traveled to Santa Fe, New Mexico. Taking their friends and relatives completely by surprise, they were married during a local fiesta. On the marriage license, Hawkins gave his real age, thirty-nine, and Graham, no doubt acutely aware of their fifteen-year age difference, subtracted eight years from her birthday, to become forty-six.

Graham in *Judith* (1950). Noguchi, who designed the set, also created Graham's headdress and jewelry.

CHAPTER TEN

Private Pains and Public Triumphs

◆

In the spring of 1950, Martha Graham and her company embarked on their first European tour with concert dates in Paris and London. The tour was a professional and personal disaster.

Graham, fifty-six, was no longer able to push her body as hard as she had before. She was suffering from painful arthritis. During one of the first performances in Paris, she injured her knee so badly that she could hardly walk. Because she was not performing, the public stopped buying tickets. When she realized that she would not be able to dance on the opening night program in London, the entire season was canceled. It took Graham eight months to recuperate from the injury, but through exercise and sheer determination, she was able to return to the stage and to go on tour again.

Hawkins and Graham's marriage was also not going well. Their relationship had always been a stormy one, for they both had strong personalities and argued constantly. Graham generally had a sunny disposition and a fine sense of humor, but like many great artists, she was self-centered and single-minded. She was notorious for her rages and outbursts of temper. She had once gotten so angry that she ripped a telephone off a wall. Before their marriage, their clashes had led to a year's separation. During the 1950 European tour it became apparent that the marriage was over. Hawkins left the company in 1951 for an independent career choreographing, teaching, and running his own troupe. He and Graham would not be divorced for four more years.

In 1951, Graham moved her studios and school, the Martha Graham School of Contemporary Dance, to its present location: a three-story turn-of-the-century brick building on Manhattan's East Sixty-third Street. Here she continued to attract students from around the world.

Graham was an uncompromising teacher. Her Puritan heritage, which stressed both discipline and freedom, was evident not only in the dances she created but in her philosophy toward the process of becoming a dancer. She believed it took ten years of training and hard work to create a dancer. It took that long to gain the flexibility and control that let a dancer exhibit both simplicity and spontaneity on stage. "I want it to look as if it's being done for the first time," she would say. This freedom could be learned only through discipline.

Graham expected no less of her students than she asked of herself. "Everyone has the right to fail," she believed. "You fail and

Graham teaching a class
(1950s)

from your failure you go up one more step—if you've got the
courage to get yourself up. There is only one cardinal sin and that
is mediocrity." But she also told her students, "a dancer must be a
realist. The toe is pointed or it is not. You are in competition with
no one but yourself. Do the work as it should be done or get out
and never come back."

Modern dance has always been an art form of individual personalities who feel compelled to express their own vision of the
world. Over the years, many of Graham's students and company
members besides Erick Hawkins and Merce Cunningham eventually struck out on their own as choreographers, dancers, and
teachers. Anna Sokolow, who danced with the Graham troupe
from 1928 to 1939, went on to establish Mexico's first modern
dance company; Pearl Lang, the first dancer that Martha ever permitted to dance one of her own roles, began an independent
career in 1952 as both a noted teacher and head of her own company; and Paul Taylor, who many consider the greatest living modern dance choreographer, formed his own company in 1961.
Younger students and dancers such as Twyla Tharp, Lar Lubovitch,

Meridith Monk, and Garth Fagan would later form their own groups to present their own visions. And some of Graham's students would make their names in fields other than dance; both Betty Ford, wife of President Gerald Ford, and rock star Madonna studied at her school.

Graham also continued to conduct her successful classes at the Neighborhood Playhouse. There she had already trained one generation of well-known actors and actresses such as Gregory Peck, Joanne Woodward, Eli Wallach, and Tony Randall. Her students would soon include future stars Woody Allen, Diane Keaton, James Caan, and Liza Minnelli.

The 1950s were a period of fierce competition between the United States and the Soviet Union. Culture was just one of the weapons used by both sides in what became known as the Cold War. Modern dance was considered a purely American art, so the U.S. State Department asked Graham, the country's most famous contemporary dancer, to become a goodwill ambassador. In February 1954, the troupe set sail for a tour of Europe that took them to England, France, Belgium, Holland, Denmark, Italy, Switzerland, and Austria. Although the weather was so frigid that the dancers had to warm up their muscles by soaking in tubs of hot water, the European tour was considered a great success.

The State Department immediately planned another trip, a sixteen-week tour of Asia and the Middle East. The group's reception on this tour was even warmer than the one they had received in Europe. The *Times* of Indonesia wrote: "If ever this paper came perilously close to forgetting its policy of leaning neither to the East nor the West, it was during Martha Graham week, because this talented woman presented something of the United States that we could wholeheartedly approve of." There was another aspect of the Graham company that could not escape attention in that part of the world: Long before the days of the civil rights movement, Graham had been the first to integrate her company. By the early 1950s, her twenty-member troupe included African-American and Asian-American dancers.

Graham, nearly sixty-two, was still performing in two or three dances each night. Her stamina was legendary. Paul Taylor, one of the dancers on the tour, wrote in his journal, "Though the rest of us wilt with the heat and sometimes drop from dysentery, she never misses a performance." And she was not only dancing. Now that Hawkins was no longer there, she was once again managing the company and conducting rehearsals. When the company returned to the States, she also gave lecture-demonstrations and taught at her school. As always, she was happiest when working.

In 1959, Graham received an invitation that surprised everyone in the worlds of modern dance and classical ballet. It came from George Balanchine (1904–1983), the noted Russian-born choreographer who was cofounder, with Lincoln Kirstein, of the New York City Ballet. Like Graham, Balanchine was a great dance innovator. He had created neoclassical ballet, a contemporary style of classical dance, a clean, streamlined technique that reflected the speed, energy, and athleticism of America, Balanchine's adopted country.

Listening to a new score (early 1960s). Although Graham did not play a musical instrument, she had a deep appreciation for music. Many of her works are danced to commissioned scores, composed specifically for her.

He had enlarged the vocabulary of classical ballet by using old steps in new ways and new steps in unexpected ways.

Balanchine wanted to work with Graham on a project that would bring their two worlds together. The idea had originally come from Lincoln Kirstein: a joint, evening-long work for both companies that would use all the orchestral music of twentieth-century Austrian composer Anton von Webern.

Episodes I and *Episodes II* turned out to be two separate sections of dance. Although both Graham and Balanchine used a few dancers from the other's company, it did not end up as a real choreographic collaboration. Graham's contribution, *Episodes I,* to Webern's more melodic, less modern sounding music, was danced by her company and four members of the City Ballet. It had elaborate decor and costumes. Graham chose to depict a dramatic historical incident: the conflict between two forceful women, Queen Elizabeth I of England and her cousin, Mary, Queen of Scots (danced by Graham), who had fought over the British crown.

Once again Graham used the narrative device of flashbacks: The ballet takes place at the moment before Mary's beheading and looks back at the events that led up to it. Graham depicted the two queens' struggle for power as an imaginary tennis match, a game that was popular in the sixteenth century, the era in which Mary and Elizabeth reigned. *Episodes II,* created by Balanchine to Webern's harsher twelve-tone music, is pure dance, an abstract, neoclassical ballet that tells no story. The dancers wear simple black and white practice clothes. Balanchine used members of his company, but gave Graham dancer Paul Taylor a twisty, pretzel-like five-minute solo.

Graham received a standing ovation before her section began, but afterward many critics thought that Balanchine's work was the more contemporary one. Although Graham dropped *Episodes I* from her company's repertoire, the evening was an important milestone in American dance history. Advocates of the two forms of dance—classical ballet and modern—would continue to argue over the merits of their respective disciplines, but a dialogue had finally been opened between the warring camps. It would not be too long before the two groups began to interact and influence each other.

Although Graham would never again work with another choreographer or dance company, she continued to collaborate with composers and with set, lighting, and costume designers. And in later years Graham would invite several stars from the world of classical ballet to dance with her troupe.

CHAPTER ELEVEN

Endings

◆

In 1960, when she was sixty-six years old, Martha Graham choreographed her 141st ballet, *Acrobats of God* (to music by Carlos Surinach), a charming, often humorous tribute to dancers, the people she referred to as "God's athletes." "Wherever a dancer stands, that spot is Holy Ground," she said. For Graham, dancing was like a religious calling. She had completely dedicated her life to it. When asked why she chose to become a dancer, she answered, "I did not choose. I was chosen." She called *Acrobats of God* "a celebration in honor of the trials and tribulations, the disciplines, denials, stringencies, glories and delights of a dancer's world."

For Graham, the coming years would indeed be filled with trials and tribulations as well as glories and delights. In 1962 and 1963, Graham and the company made triumphant tours of Europe and the Middle East. In Israel, she helped Bethsabee de Rothschild start a school to train students in her style and establish that country's first modern dance troupe—the Batsheva Dance Company—to perform her works. A similar school and company, the London Contemporary Dance Ensemble, was founded by English admirers at this time as well. Graham continued to receive honorary degrees, awards, and accolades for her work.

Many of the people who had been important to her, however, were gone. Her mother, with whom she had remained very close, had died in 1958. Her oldest friend, her former companion and collaborator, Louis Horst, died in 1964. In 1967, another longtime friend and collaborator, lighting designer Jean Rosenthal, died after a long illness. Her patron, Bethsabee de Rothschild, moved to Tel Aviv to devote all her time, energy, and money to the Batsheva Dance Company.

Graham herself was not well. She called this period in her life the time of "black despair." Her arthritis was worse than ever. As she had done as a child in Allegheny, she wore gloves whenever she went out. But this time it was to hide her hands, which were twisted by the crippling disease. Dancing alone and unsupported was nearly impossible; she was not strong enough to conduct daily classes. She suffered bouts of depression during which she would not leave her apartment to attend rehearsals. For a time she was abusing alcohol to make herself forget her fears and anxieties about the future. But as always, Graham was able to draw on her inner strength to overcome obstacles. Her health improved enough for her to appear on stage again. On May 15, 1968, at the age of seventy-four, Graham gave one of her last dance performances in *A Time of Snow* (to music by Dello Joio), a ballet about the famous lovers of medieval legend, Abelard and Heloise. They are seen in their old age looking back on their lives.

After she retired from the stage Graham no longer made dances that had strong female characters as their center, perhaps because she could not bring those roles to life herself. As early as the late 1940s, other dancers in the company had been taking over the roles that Graham had made famous but could no longer dance. It was extremely difficult, however, for her to give up a part, because she always thought of herself as a performer, not a choreographer. "I think I really only started to choreograph so that I could have something to show off in," she wrote late in life. "It came as a great shock to me when I stopped dancing that I was honored for my choreography as well." In 1991, in one of her last interviews, she told a reporter, "I would much rather be dancing. I will always miss it."

She went on making dances, although at a much slower pace than before. She also continued to give eloquent precurtain talks and lecture-demonstrations about her life and work. She was as charismatic and dramatic a speaker as she had been a dancer. Her mere presence on a theater stage filled audiences with a sense of electric anticipation. Graham's appearance had changed little over the past decades. Her masklike face, with its high, hollow cheekbones and intense, blazing eyes, was unlined. For many years she had worn her straight black hair pulled back and piled high, arranged with ornamental pins and headdresses. She liked to wear kimonolike robes or glittering gold lamé gowns. Although small in stature, Graham had a deep resonant voice, and like the great actress she was, she always projected a powerful presence.

In 1969, the company had their last New York season for four years. During the next few years, Graham was very ill and was hospitalized several times. By the spring of 1973, however, she had recovered sufficiently to resume duties as director of her school, to choreograph, and to publish her notebooks, containing thoughts and philosophy about her life's work. That season, the Martha Graham Dance Company once again performed on Broadway; the next year, Graham was well enough to travel with the troupe on another successful tour of Europe. In 1975, they became the first modern dance troupe to have a season at New York's prestigious Metropolitan Opera House. The following year, Graham became the first dance personality to receive the Presidential Medal of Freedom, the country's highest civilian award. In the

Ballet superstars Rudolf Nureyev and Margot Fonteyn chat with Graham and First Lady Betty Ford (a former Graham student) at a gala performance in 1975.

proclamation, President Gerald Ford called her "a national treasure."

World renowned, Graham attracted international celebrities who wanted to work with her. Three of classical ballet's superstars, Rudolf Nureyev, Margot Fonteyn, and Mikhail Baryshnikov, danced with her company. Singer-actress Liza Minnelli took the speaking role in Graham's comic 1978 work, *The Owl and the Pussycat* (to music by Surinach), a ballet based on Edward Lear's nonsense poem. Actress Kathleen Turner was The One Who Speaks in a revival of *Letter to the World*. Fashion designers Halston and Calvin Klein helped finance new ballets and also created costumes for her company.

In 1985, Graham accepted a position on the National Council on the Arts, the advisory board of the National Endowment for the Arts, the government agency that awards grants to artists. That year she also traveled with her company to the Paris Opera, where they became the first American dance troupe to perform on the stage that was the home of the world's oldest classical ballet company. Graham was made a Knight of the French Legion of Honor by the government, just one of the forty honors and awards from around the world that she received in her lifetime.

Despite her ill health, Graham continued to work on new dances whenever she was able. She oversaw rehearsals, reconstructed and restored older pieces, and helped her assistants preserve her work on tape and film. She was also writing her autobiography, which would be published in 1991.

Graham in her prized antique
red lacquered Chinese bed
(1964)

Graham's last complete work, *Maple Leaf Rag,* premiered on
October 2, 1990, during the company's New York season. The
music she chose was the playful, syncopated ragtime of Scott
Joplin, the very tunes Louis Horst had played to cheer her so many
years before. In December, Graham accompanied her dancers on a
fifty-five-day tour of the Far East, but her deteriorating health
forced her to return home.

Martha Graham died on April 1, 1991, in New York City, from
complications from pneumonia. She was a few weeks shy of her
ninety-seventh birthday. Before her final illness, she had been at
work on *The Eye of the Goddess,* "a journey through time" commissioned by the government of Spain to celebrate the five hundredth
anniversary of Columbus's voyages to America. It seemed a fitting
last subject for Martha Graham, another intrepid explorer who
had, long ago, set out on her own lifelong journey of discovery.

EPILOGUE

◆

Since Martha Graham's death, her school has continued without her, as has the Martha Graham Dance Company. Her company, which celebrates its seventieth anniversary in 1996, is the oldest continuously performing modern dance troupe in the world.

Martha Graham, who in her lifetime created nearly two hundred works of dance, was a living legend. The legacy she left to the worlds of dance and theater was immense. She created a style of her own, a new language of dance, an original way of communicating through movement, which has been accepted around the world. She developed a training method that could be passed down and taught to others, a method as systematic as classical ballet. She founded a school and taught and influenced generations of dancers, choreographers, and actors. "I'd like to be known as a storyteller," Graham once said, and she conceived a new kind of theater, plays that fused words and music, decor and movement.

Her innovations in costume and set design were adopted by Broadway and the opera as well as dance.

Martha Graham was an adventurer, a risk taker undeterred by critics or audiences, who did not always understand her work. Throughout her life, she was considered a groundbreaker, changing the way people thought about dance and theater. She gave everything to her art and never compromised her work in order to be more popular. Agnes de Mille called her "the most unpredictable, the most searching, the most radical of all choreographers." But Graham never saw herself in this light. In a 1980 speech, she said, "I was not a revolutionary at all. I just walked a little further." But in her electrifying performances and in the brilliant dances she created, she challenged audiences to look within themselves, to courageously and honestly confront their fears and biases, their hopes and loves—to be, in short, better human beings.

BIBLIOGRAPHY

◆

Anderson, Jack. *Ballet and Modern Dance: A Concise History*. Princeton, N.J.: Princeton Book Company, 1986.

de Mille, Agnes. *The Book of Dance*. New York: Golden, 1963.

————. *Martha: The Life and Works of Martha Graham*. New York: Random House, 1991.

Fonteyn, Margot. *The Magic of Dance*. New York: Knopf, 1979.

Graham, Martha. *Blood Memory*. Garden City, N.Y.: Doubleday, 1991.

————. *The Notebooks of Martha Graham*. New York: Harcourt, Brace, Jovanovitch, 1973.

Horosko, Marian. *Martha Graham: The Evolution of Her Dance Theory and Training, 1926–1991*. Pennington, N.J. and Chicago: Chicago Review Press, 1991.

Leatherman, Leroy, with photos by Martha Swope. *Portrait of the Lady as an Artist*. New York: Knopf, 1966.

Lloyd, Margaret. *The Borzoi Book of Modern Dance.* New York: Knopf, 1949.

McDonagh, Don. *Complete Guide to Modern Dance.* New York: Popular Library, 1977.

————. *Martha Graham: A Biography.* New York: Praeger, 1973.

Morgan, Barbara. *Martha Graham: 16 Dances in Photos.* Duell, N.Y.: Sloan and Pearce, 1941.

Noguchi, Isamu. *A Sculptor's World.* New York: Harper & Row, 1968.

———— and Tobi Tobias. *Oral History Project.* New York: New York Public Library Dance Collection, 1979.

Stodelle, Ernestine. *Deep Song: The Dance Story of Martha Graham.* New York: Schermer, 1984.

Terry, Walter. *Frontiers of Dance: The Life of Martha Graham.* New York: Crowell, 1974.

INDEX